Tiny Tales

North West England

First published in Great Britain in 2007 by
Young Writers, Remus House, Coltsfoot Drive,
Peterborough, PE2 9JX
Tel (01733) 890066 Fax (01733) 313524
All Rights Reserved

© Copyright Contributors 2007
SB ISBN 978-1-84431-314-3

Disclaimer
Young Writers has maintained every effort
to publish stories that will not cause offence.
Any stories, events or activities relating to individuals
should be read as fictional pieces and not construed
as real-life character portrayal.

Foreword

Young Writers was established in 1991, with the aim of encouraging the children and young adults of today to think and write creatively. Our latest primary school competition, *Tiny Tales*, posed an exciting challenge for these young authors: to write, in no more than fifty words, a story encompassing a beginning, a middle and an end. We call this the mini saga.

Tiny Tales North West England is our latest offering from the wealth of young talent that has mastered this incredibly challenging form. With such an abundance of imagination, humour and ability evident in such a wide variety of stories, these young writers cannot fail to enthral and excite with every tale.

Contents

Abbott Community Primary School, Collyhurst
Shanice Bailey (11) 13
Nathan Smith (11) 14
Karl Harvey (11) 15
Katie Stewart (11) 16
Anthony Melbourne (11) 17

Austin Friars St Monica's School, Carlisle
Hannah McMillan (9) 18

Boarshaw Community Primary School, Middleton
Molly Sullivan (9) 19
Rebekah Hilton (9) 20
Alisha Thompson-Arif (10) 21
Morgan McFadyen (10) 22
Dominic Kosylo (11) 23
Talha Ali (11) 24
Chloe Murphy (10) 25
Imarnie Suleman-Lee (10) 26

Cherry Manor Primary School, Sale
Callum Taylor (11) 27
Rebecca Perkins (11) 28

Amy Woolley (11) 29
Melisa Bajric (11) 30
Cara Shenton (11) 31
Laura Doorbar (9) 32
Liam Bates (11) 33
Milly Daniels (10) 34

Christ Church Primary School, Birkenhead
Harry Roche (9) 35
Charlotte Holmes (9) 36
Chloe Griffiths (11) 37
Samira Asmar (11) 38

Goodly Dale Primary School, Windermere
Amanda Mellish (11) 39
Becky Wilkinson (11) 40
Abigail Whitney (10) 41
Joshua Quinn (10) 42
Charlotte Graves (11) 43
Troy Hinton-Winrow (10) 44

Hale CE Primary School, Liverpool
Annabel Wardrop (9) 45
Christopher Prince (9) 46
Zoey Davies (9) 47

Thomas Henesy (9)	48
Rebecca Scott (9)	49
Lewis Bowen (9)	50
Sian Whiteley (9)	51
Reece Clarke (9)	52
Albie Knowles (9)	53
Tom Dennis (8)	54
James Hilton (8)	55
Eleanor Powell (9)	56
Charlotte Babarinsa (9)	57
Paige Hymas (8)	58
Gabriella Evans (9)	59

Ivegill School, Carlisle

Hugh Law (9)	60
Andrew Tyson (8)	61
Mary Tyson (9)	62
David Leigh (9)	63
Hannah Craig (8)	64
Richard Woods (9)	65
Joseph Armstrong (8)	66

Mablins Lane Primary School, Crewe

Josh Tomkinson (10)	67
Rhys Hodges (10)	68
Sophie Cherrington (10)	69
Georgina Rodwell (10)	70
Jack Price	71
Carla Harding (10)	72
Laura Spence (10)	73
John Murphy (9)	74

Alex Banks (10)	75
Rebecca Leeke (10)	76
Shane Checkman (10)	77
Emily Bell (10)	78
Rebekah-Jayne Bradley (10)	79
Andrew Bennett (10)	80
Tanya Ross (10)	81
Ryan Brogan (10)	82
Charles Pointon (10)	83
Chloe Tomkinson (9)	84
James Owen (10)	85
Adam Bartlem (10)	86
Katie Brown (9)	87
Amy Billington (10)	88
Lucy King	89
Gemma Warrington (10)	90
Ashleigh Clarke	91
Chloe Holland	92
Keegan Barnford (9)	93
Matthew Minshull	94
Josh Long	95
Calum Dutton (10)	96
Thomas Oldham (10)	97
Stacey Herring (10)	98
Lauren Griffin (9)	99
Robbie Handley	100
Anna Harrison (10)	101
Rebecca Boyd	102
George Blythe (10)	103

Monton Green Primary School, Eccles

Lucy Greenall (9)	104
Rebecca Dooley (9)	105
Jessica Sweeney (9)	106
Rebecca Hill (9)	107
Lauren Willetts (9)	108
Paige Royle (9)	109
Daniel Wilson (9)	110
Kallen Chapman (9)	111

Our Lady of Pity RC Primary School, Greasby

Lydia Power	112

Plumpton Primary School, Penrith

Jack Forster (11)	113
Richard Sykes (11)	114
Harry Hogarth (10)	115
Samantha Bell (9)	116

Portland Primary School, Birkenhead

Natasha Burns (8)	117

St Alban's Catholic Primary School, Macclesfield

Thomas Healey (10)	118
Emily Wardle (11)	119
Tom Ridings (10)	120
Megan Quigley (10)	121
Andrew Loxham (11)	122

Hannah Brennan	123
Anna Mattock (11)	124
Megan Clowes (11)	125
Jake Taylor (11)	126
Rachael Perkins (11)	127
László Zörényi (11)	128
Kevin Wright (11)	129
Christopher Weetman (11)	130
Rachel Horner (11)	131
Nicholas Phillips (10)	132
Jonathan Thompson (10)	133
Lauren Smethurst (11)	134
Aidan Smith (11)	135
Arran McCloskey (11)	136
Robert Nowak (11)	137
Callum Byrne (11)	138
Michael Jennings (11)	139
Mark Elkommos (11)	140
Jack Pritchard (11)	141
Anna Harrington (11)	142
Jake Turner (10)	143
Thomas Kaye (11)	144
Matthew McFahn (11)	145
Thomas Priest (10)	146

St Bega's CE Primary School, Holmrook

Sarah Hooper (8)	147
Abigail Cookman (10)	148
Emily Tyson (10)	149
Emma Thornley (9)	150

Jessica Harrison 151

St Gilbert's RC Primary School, Eccles
Emma Riley (9) 152
Liam McCusker (9) 153
Amy Ruddle (9) 154
Tom Mosey (9) 155
Charlotte Stoddard (9) 156
Sarah Garratt (9) 157
Emily Devine (9) 158
Erin Clemans (9) 159
Alex Rogers (9) 160
Ruby Howard (9) 161
Molly Glynn-Whitehead (9) 162
Eleanor Dean (8) 163
George Hughes (9) 164
Leah Glynn (9) 165
Lucy O'Reilly (8) 166
Tom Nuttall (9) 167

St Gregory's Catholic Primary School, Workington
Rachel Kenyon (11) 168
Daniel Robinson (11) 169
Jaye Poland (10) 170
Amelia-Jane Gregory (11) 171
Lindsey Kelly (10) 172
Sarah Robertson (11) 173
Niall Bainbridge (10) 174
Rachel Carter (11) 175
Chelsia Austin (11) 176

Ryan Allenby (11) 177

St Laurence's Catholic Primary School, Liverpool
James Simpson (11) 178
Emmi Gee (11) 179
Antonia Gorman (11) 180
Chloe Atherton (11) 181
Dominic Castell (11) 182
Megan Egan (11) 183
Adam Campbell (11) 184
Holly Hughes (11) 185
Shelley Blackburn (11) 186
Jadeine Fagan (11) 187
Kay Bell (11) 188
Samantha Nairn (11) 189
Aimeé Halleron (11) 190
Paul Richmond (11) 191
Lauren McArdle (11) 192
Kevin Furlong (11) 193
Sian Bradshaw (11) 194
Ben Dillon (11) 195
Jake Lunt (11) 196
Emily Canning (11) 197
Aidan Watkinson (11) 198
Callum Conning (11) 199
Laura Brown (11) 200
Stephanie Stuart (11) 201
Bradley O'Connor (11) 202
Keeley Porter (11) 203

St Luke's RC Primary School, Frodsham

Ronce Carl N Saputil (11)	204
Victoria Garner (11)	205
Ellie Ford (11)	206
Emma-Louise Pyatt (11)	207
Lauren Creamer (11)	208
Abigail Dimelow (10)	209
Faith Howley (11)	210
Jamie Milne (11)	211
Emily Mann (11)	212
James Martin (11)	213
Charlotte Read (10)	214
Charlotte Rose (11)	215
Adam Webb (10)	216

St Philip's CE Primary School, Liverpool

Caitlin Baxendale (10)	217
Natalie Baker (10)	218
Lauren Keegan (10)	219
Jessica Taylor (9)	220
Amy Perrin (10)	221
Stacey Forrestil (10)	222
Megan Smith (10)	223
Craig Collins (10)	224
Amy-Jo Tyrrell (10)	225
Amy Thomas (10)	226
Neil Seddon (10)	227
Liam Morrison (10)	228
Brandon Cannell (10)	229
Luke Straiton (10)	230

St Stephen's CE Primary School, Banks

Melanie Grandidge (9)	231
Anthony Pilcher (9)	232
Corey Flannery (9)	233
Luke Evans (9)	234
Laura Jones (9)	235
Richard Gaskell (9)	236
Bradley Garton (9)	237
Ryan Ousey (9)	238
Louis Wright (9)	239
Charlotte Smith (9)	240
Cameron Williams (9)	241
Joshua Moniz (9)	242
Bryony Fitzpatrick (9)	243
Kyle Ruscoe (9)	244
Sophie Stevens (9)	245
Amy Gillow (9)	246
Lilyanna Rigby (9)	247
Leah Gearie (8)	248
Connor Hancock (8)	249

St Teresa's Primary School, St Helen's

Siobhan Glover (10)	250
Daniel Shepherd (9)	251
Natalie Devine (10)	252
Katie Ellis (9)	253
Daniel Eddleston (10)	254
Nathan Baines (10)	255

Sound & District Primary School, Sound

Beth Holmes (11)	256

Leanne Read (10) 257
Andrew Elson (10) 258
Lucy Earls (9) 259
Becky Hadwen (10) 260
Connor Thundercliffe (10) 261
Ollie Barnes (9)...262
Katie Johnson (10) 263
Jordan Edge (10) 264

South Walney Junior School, Walney
Connor McGowan (11)..............................265
Rachel Pearce (11)...................................266
Bradley Jepson-Leech (10).......................267
Matthew Williamson (11)...........................268
Lauren Devlin (11) 269
Abby Long (10)..270
Jayd Arnold (11) 271
Hannah Livoooy (11) 272
Rebecca Murdoch (11) 273
Callum Sparkes (11)..................................274
Emily Bosanko (11) 275
Harry Winship (11).....................................276
Natasha Reay (11) 277
Natalie Jayne White (11) 278
Sasha McCormick (11) 279
Jodie Evans (10) 280
Phoebe Goulding (11)................................281
Joshua Francis (11)...................................282
Vicky Rigg (11) 283
Rebecca Reid (10) 284

Hannah Faragher (11)...............................285
Welton Primary School, Carlisle
Catherine Stobart (10)...............................286
Zoe Morris (8)..287
Michael Studholme (10) 288
Megan Wetherell (11) 289
Sarah Wolstencroft (9)...............................290

The Mini Sagas

The Attack Of Nessie

Help! The Loch Ness monster was coming towards me. I tried to fight it off, but I couldn't! I froze to the spot. I discovered that it wasn't coming to kill me, it was coming to wake me up from this terrible dream. Anyway it was just my mum!

Shanice Bailey (11)
Abbott Community Primary School, Collyhurst

My Missing Hamster

There it was crawling up my arm. Then suddenly it crawled down my back. I woke up with horror and turned round. I could feel something nibbling at my toes. Then my mum shouted, 'Nathan the hamster's gone missing.'

Nathan Smith (11)
Abbott Community Primary School, Collyhurst

Bathtub Splash

There she was, driving into the sea because she has no brakes, screaming for help. *Splash!* into the water she went. She started drowning, trying to get back to the top of the sea, swimming for her life to get out.
'Sheela, get up, you're asleep in the bath.'

Karl Harvey (11)
Abbott Community Primary School, Collyhurst

Got You

Flower knew something had happened as soon as she stepped through that front door. But what? She did not understand why Summer was just laying on the bathroom floor. Flower crept nervously over to Summer.
'Got you!' shouted Summer, crying with laughter as she jumped to her feet.

Katie Stewart (11)
Abbott Community Primary School, Collyhurst

A Bad Dream

Me, Steven and Daniel were getting chased by vampires. Steven was hit and down. The vampires started to bite him. Then he turned into a zombie. I was the only one left. Then I heard, 'David wake up, you are going to be late for school.'

Anthony Melbourne (11)
Abbott Community Primary School, Collyhurst

Jene Was Worried

Jene was worried about going grey. She tried everything she could but it wouldn't go away. One day Jene found a grey hair. She said, 'Argh, I'm getting old. I know, I'll take it out.' But she kept doing it and became bald. So she got a wig.

Hannah McMillan (9)
Austin Friars St Monica's School, Carlisle

Surprise!

Marian was worried because it was Christmas Eve and she had not written a letter to Father Christmas for the toys she wanted and her family said absolutely nothing to her that day when she was worried. The next day, 'Surprise!' All the family were there in front of her.

Molly Sullivan (9)
Boarshaw Community Primary School, Middleton

The New Roller Coaster

One day three friends went to the fair. They were having so much fun until someone said no one could go on the roller coaster. The friends were disappointed until they saw a new ride. It was bigger than the other. They went on it and had some fun.

Rebekah Hilton (9)
Boarshaw Community Primary School, Middleton

Surprise Party

One night the cat and fiddle went outside, it was Cow's birthday. Everyone wanted to throw a surprise party. Cat played a birthday song, Dog came with presents, Spoon made the cake and then Cow came. She came out and got such a surprise she jumped over the moon.

Alisha Thompson-Arif (10)
Boarshaw Community Primary School, Middleton

The Two Best Friends

Donna was going bowling for Katie's birthday. They got there and were ready to play. They were both very excited. They played and Donna sadly did not win, Katie did, but because they were best friends that did not really matter to them.

Morgan McFadyen (10)
Boarshaw Community Primary School, Middleton

The Missing Boy

The house was creepy and scary. A young boy called Roger was a nosy, cunning boy. He always wondered what was in the spooky house. One gloomy day he decided to have a little peek in the house. He opened the door and was grabbed in and never seen again.

Dominic Kosylo (11)
Boarshaw Community Primary School, Middleton

Mr Lion

Once upon a time there was a very brave lion. He didn't have any food or money and was very upset. 'Everyone's got money - I'm the only person who hasn't.'
One morning he woke to discover a bag of gold coins and he could buy food again and was happy.

Talha Ali (11)
Boarshaw Community Primary School, Middleton

Surprise

Mia was astonished. She thought everyone had forgotten her birthday! That day as she was walking home from school a tear dripped down her cheek because she was a teenager that day, not even her friends said anything. She went home, it was silent … everyone came up and shouted … 'Surprise!'

Chloe Murphy (10)
Boarshaw Community Primary School, Middleton

Untitled

In the science lab Tyra was working on her spells. Suddenly the spell went wrong and turned her teacher into a frog! Tyra panicked and examined the book - she had to kiss him! She was the only one who could, she'd cast the spell. They kissed, the spell was broken.

Imarnie Suleman-Lee (10)
Boarshaw Community Primary School, Middleton

The Warehouse Gang

Luke heard a noise so he went up to investigate. He was just about to open the door. He felt terrified because he didn't know what was behind the door. He opened the door and looked around and saw a gang sitting in the corner drinking and smoking. Oh no!

Callum Taylor (11)
Cherry Manor Primary School, Sale

The Old Church

Lucy felt something touch her on the shoulder, she screamed so loud. Lucy and Sam started to look about the church and then she felt someone touch her again so she turned around. No one was there. And then she looked again. There was a vampire there behind her.

Rebecca Perkins (11)
Cherry Manor Primary School, Sale

A Nervous Wreck

The door flew open. A gust of wind skimmed my face. I walked into a plain room, there was silence. Suddenly blood gushed down the old damp walls as if they were human. I was a nervous wreck, so I ran into the next room. My heart skipped 10 beats.

Amy Woolley (11)
Cherry Manor Primary School, Sale

The Dad Catcher!

'Hurry up!' Summer shouted. The man ran quickly behind them. His chubby cheeks bright red.

'Argh!' The girls shouted. The man wrapped his hairy arms around them.

'I want you to clean your rooms!' After all it was just their dad.

Melisa Bajric (11)
Cherry Manor Primary School, Sale

The Mansion

The children were so silent you could hear a pin drop. They were shocked at the super spooky mansion. The children, still shocked, had the most strange instincts to walk up the drive to the mansion. The door swung open and the children were flung in with a scream. 'Argh!'

Cara Shenton (11)
Cherry Manor Primary School, Sale

You're Not Alone

As Lara entered the heart of the castle the atmosphere changed. It was warm and welcoming, not dark, lonely and cold. The stone walls changed to blood-red and the mud floor to red brick. Then a door flung open. Lara wasn't alone.

Laura Doorbar (9)
Cherry Manor Primary School, Sale

Church Who?

One spooky night in the village, one of the villagers heard a noise coming from Spookhead Church. So he went to check, but everything was fine. The next night was Freaky Friday. Friday 13th - he heard it again. He went to check it out. He got to the doors … 'Argh!'

Liam Bates (11)
Cherry Manor Primary School, Sale

Full Moon

A bloodthirsty werewolf crawled towards the church. The vicar shook. He ran. But not fast enough. He was ripped up, all of his bones licked clean of blood. The werewolf howled in delight. He was like this for another 70 years.

Milly Daniels (10)
Cherry Manor Primary School, Sale

The Aliens' Short Story

Late at night I could hear strange noises. I looked out of the window. I could see something flashing outside. I went to investigate, it was an alien's spacecraft. When I got closer the aliens spotted me. They got scared and flew away into the night sky.

Harry Roche (9)
Christ Church Primary School, Birkenhead

A Friendly Abduction

Lancaster invaded by aliens. I was terrified. We all ran and I fell. He came towards me, his green curly arms reached out. I thought he would take me aboard his ship but he said, 'Can I help you?'
'Come and play,' I said to my new friend.

Charlotte Holmes (9)
Christ Church Primary School, Birkenhead

Home At Last

'I can't wait until we get home Mum!' Clara exclaimed. Clara was on her way home from Paris.
'I loved it there, I don't know why you want to come home,' her mum said. They finally arrived home.
'Oh, we're home!' Clara said.
'Home at last!' they all said together.

Chloe Griffiths (11)
Christ Church Primary School, Birkenhead

Wrong Again

This time my experiment couldn't go wrong. But the blood drained from my face as the test tube containing the concoction began to tremble. The crimson liquid was frothing and rising rapidly, bubbling over the surface onto the floor. Well, I won't be getting any more pocket money for awhile …

Samira Asmar (11)
Christ Church Primary School, Birkenhead

Mountain Troll

I crumple my poor nose to the horrid smell coming along the deserted corridor. My sapphire blue eyes stinging with the stench of … Mountain Troll. A statue of Bloodworth the Barmy is where I'm hidden behind. I hear the troll grunting past my petrified self. I'm breathing slowly. Help me!

Amanda Mellish (11)
Goodly Dale Primary School, Windermere

Heaven And Hell

The thick heavy mud squelched as I trudged through the battlefield. Blood and pain started to seep out of my head. All the sounds of bombing and shooting began to fade away. The brightness of the daylight started to become dimmer and darker, as I ascended to the places unknown!

Becky Wilkinson (11)
Goodly Dale Primary School, Windermere

The Sinking Sand

The beach awaited. Looking down, I noticed my feet had disappeared. I was sinking! Soon it was round my ankles, up to my waist, my shoulders! It was grasping my neck! I was strangled, dying! This oozy sinking sand was taking my …
'Dylan get out of that muddy puddle now!'

Abigail Whitney (10)
Goodly Dale Primary School, Windermere

Fighter Jet Dream

I was alone in my U18 Raptor fighter jet plane, there was heavy rain. I felt an adrenaline rush as I entered the battle, my stomach wrenched suddenly as a rocket hit the rear fuselage, my plane took a nosedive as I pulled the ejector handle strongly. *Battle time!*

Joshua Quinn (10)
Goodly Dale Primary School, Windermere

Rabbit Dumpty

There once lived a rabbit, Rabbit Dumpty. One thing Dumpty wanted to do was go through the magical door over the road. After his dinner, he skipped to the magical door and whispered, 'Won't harm anyone stepping through the door.' He suddenly heard his mum saying, 'No!' as he fell …

Charlotte Graves (11)
Goodly Dale Primary School, Windermere

The Kid In The Tree

Up to the top he climbs, to the top of the tree he climbs. To the tip of the top he climbs, he's at the top of the tree. He looks down, the ground is a mile away. Down he jumps, down to the ground. Oh, the solid ground. Safety!

Troy Hinton-Winrow (10)
Goodly Dale Primary School, Windermere

Fuzzy Wuzzy

One night I couldn't sleep. A star shot past my skylight. It came to Earth. A tiny, pink, fluffy alien emerged and crept into my room saying, 'Hello, my name is Ivan!'
We went into his spaceship.
Suddenly he bit me, threw me out, thankfully I landed on my trampoline.

Annabel Wardrop (9)
Hale CE Primary School, Liverpool

Titanic

I stood at the bow of the Titanic. I heard a noise. The ship was jerking and sinking, people were pushing, I fell into the water, holding my breath. The ship fell on top of me. I was sinking down … I woke in fright after falling off my top bunk.

Christopher Prince (9)
Hale CE Primary School, Liverpool

The Wet Walk

One day I was walking. When I had been walking for an hour I found a river. Someone called my name, 'Zoey!'
I felt a tap on my shoulder. I fell in, the river splashed me. Why was it soapy? Just then I woke up. I was in the bath!

Zoey Davies (9)
Hale CE Primary School, Liverpool

Night Flight

A windy night, I was flying a Boeing 747 to Australia. 500 people onboard. Suddenly, lightning struck the left wing, the plane bounced to its right, lightning hit the fuel tank. Fuel was leaking from the jet. I saw the Sydney Opera House.
Suddenly the engines came to life - safe.

Thomas Henesy (9)
Hale CE Primary School, Liverpool

The Safari Park

On our way through the safari park, we went in the lion enclosure. The car stopped, so we got out and pushed. Suddenly in the corner of my eye I saw an enormous shadow of a viscous lion … I turned in fright to find a small cub licking my feet.

Rebecca Scott (9)
Hale CE Primary School, Liverpool

The Big Problem

I was on the Black Pearl when the Kracken came up behind me and bit my bottom. Then he swallowed me. It was a good job I was peppered otherwise it wouldn't have spit me out. I threw a barrel of gunpowder in his mouth. *Bang!* It blew.

Lewis Bowen (9)
Hale CE Primary School, Liverpool

King Henry VIII

Here I am. A stag running away from King Henry's hands. They are on hunt. I am the hunted. King Henry's feared sword is drawn. The hounds are barking. My heart's pumping, it can't slow down. Will I faint? I find a cave to hide in … I'm safe. For now.

Sian Whiteley (9)
Hale CE Primary School, Liverpool

Summer Storm

I was driving in Mexico during a wild storm. Wind-blown trees fell, making me swerve. Suddenly the car tipped. The door opened, I fell on the hard dusty road. I heard a roaring noise coming closer. It was a big red truck … *Bang!* I fell out of bed, *bump!*

Reece Clarke (9)
Hale CE Primary School, Liverpool

The Rude Awakening

I was at Anfield playing Liverpool against Everton. I was playing up front. Lesscot booted the ball at my face. The first aid stretcher men came on and brought me off. It was a dream. My dad was waking me up for school. He was slapping me on my face.

Albie Knowles (9)
Hale CE Primary School, Liverpool

A Fierce Giant

I climbed up a beanstalk and crept by the giant's house. I heard him roar, 'Fee fi fo fum!' I turned and tried to escape but the beanstalk was too slippery.
I felt the giant pulling me back, I shouted, 'Help!'
But the giant asked, 'Do you want some tea?'

Tom Dennis (8)
Hale CE Primary School, Liverpool

Cliffhanger

I anxiously stood on the edge of the cliff, my heart was beating faster and faster. My legs were shaking and my mouth felt dry. Suddenly, a hand pushed hard on my shoulder and I fell … down … hair blowing, until I felt my bungee rope pull my ankles skyward.

James Hilton (8)
Hale CE Primary School, Liverpool

The Noise

One day a boy and girl were looking for their auntie's mansion. Their names were Jessica and Dave. They were cold and starving. Worse still, they heard a noise coming from the bushes, they were petrified, it was coming closer, they started running faster ... it was only a mouse. 'Argh!'

Eleanor Powell (9)
Hale CE Primary School, Liverpool

Night At The Museum

One day I was visiting the Maritime Museum. I was travelling round when ... suddenly I found no one was there. I was scared. Was everything going to come to life? The light turned off. It was dark. Something moved, I turned to find the dinosaur skeleton wanting to play 'fetch'.

Charlotte Babarinsa (9)
Hale CE Primary School, Liverpool

A Stranger?

When I was playing out I saw a man I thought I'd never seen before. He came towards me, getting closer, my heart was thumping faster and faster, I thought he was going to take me away ... terrified ... I realised it was my dad coming to call me for tea.

Paige Hymas (8)
Hale CE Primary School, Liverpool

Bungee Jump

I got carried up in the cage of the bungee jump. They were strapping me in. I got to the top, then I tiptoed nervously. The gate opened, then suddenly I jumped. I felt the rope coming apart. It snapped. In horror I woke, I had fallen out of bed.

Gabriella Evans (9)
Hale CE Primary School, Liverpool

Bombs Over London

One dark night in World War II the searchlights were on in London. The enemy came over and dropped their bombs. A little five-year-old girl just escaped. Crying and running around the little homeless girl cried for help. A civilian took her to a camp outside London.

Hugh Law (9)
Ivegill School, Carlisle

Bombs Over Britain

One day in the Second World War the enemy bombed a little girl's house. Her parents died, she was five years old. The little girl lay in a civilian man's arms. The civilian was a really kind old man. He looked after the child for the rest of her life.

Andrew Tyson (8)
Ivegill School, Carlisle

Upsetting Moments

Two and a half years ago, a five-year-old's mother died. Her father was trying to comfort her. Russia was at war. Natasha's father was a retired officer of the army. He was old and going to die one day soon. Was there anyone left to look after her?

Mary Tyson (9)
Ivegill School, Carlisle

One Man War

One night when I was sitting on the bench I saw my dad was actually going to war, and I started to cry because I did not think he would make it through the war. This guard came along and picked me up and I told him all about it.

David Leigh (9)
Ivegill School, Carlisle

Where's Mummy Gone?

My darling daughter and I had been held captive. All I had was her, my clothing and some small rounded objects in my pocket. She was screaming through her tears so badly I could barely understand what she was saying, it was something like, 'Where's Mummy gone?' Mummy was dead.

Hannah Craig (8)
Ivegill School, Carlisle

Disastrous Girl

A small girl hugging her dad. Crying as she put her sweet hands around him. She saw her dad's eyes gleaming. The girl had not seen her dad for years. She could feel his soft coat. He was sweaty from his hideous war. She was delighted to see her dad.

Richard Woods (9)
Ivegill School, Carlisle

The Kidnappers

Two people sitting on a seat. A little girl screaming her head off, because an old man had kidnapped her to be his daughter. Her parents were in bed, it was 12 o'clock at night. 'Be quiet little girl,' threatened the old man. What happens next? You decide and tell me.

Joseph Armstrong (8)
Ivegill School, Carlisle

Monster

I heard a noise. *What was it?* I thought, *could it be that monster that scared the daylights out of me yesterday?* The door slammed shut, I was scared now. 'Go away!' I said. I heard another noise, what was it?
I heard something get closer and said, 'Hi!'

Josh Tomkinson (10)
Mablins Lane Primary School, Crewe

Last Term

On the coast of England there's a school. It's end of term. The boys go to the cliff. Takes you to the forest.
The day before the end of year I saw something come out the forest. The next day I looked again in the forest it was my friends.

Rhys Hodges (10)
Mablins Lane Primary School, Crewe

Screamed

It was big, it was dry, the sweat went down my spine. It was the massive ride in my eyes. It was 'The Digger'. 'Come on Sam.'
My friend said, 'No, I'll wait down here for you.'
It was my turn. I screamed as I went down.

Sophie Cherrington (10)
Mablins Lane Primary School, Crewe

Diddy And Daisy: Cake Mystery!

Diddy and Daisy were sitting in the tent eating fairy cakes. Diddy ate ten and Daisy ate 32, but then Diddy was sick all over the rest, and then Daisy kicked her in the leg. Diddy woke up from a dream and there were cakes all over her bed.

Georgina Rodwell (10)
Mablins Lane Primary School, Crewe

The Creeper

It was night and it crept on me, I felt it climbing. I ran but it was almost too late. It crept on me. I started slapping myself. It kept going. It reached my neck. I looked around and it was my mum tickling me with a feather duster.

Jack Price
Mablins Lane Primary School, Crewe

The Long Journey

I am frightened. I want to get it, I really do. It's raining bad. I'm soaked. It's only one mile away. I've already walked two miles! Nearly there now. Entering building, I'm waiting for lift. Now I'm on. *Boom!* I'm there in the interview room getting an excellent job!

Carla Harding (10)
Mablins Lane Primary School, Crewe

Footsteps

I was walking home. Someone was behind me. I could hear their footsteps. I ran, the footsteps ran. As I slowed down the footsteps slowed down, I was scared, I had goosebumps everywhere, my throat went dry. Oh it's the echo of my own footsteps!

Laura Spence (10)
Mablins Lane Primary School, Crewe

Christmas Bug

Billy and his mum went to the shopping mall at Christmas.
'It's going to be a Christmas out of this world,' shouted Mum. Later that night, at midnight, a flying saucer landed on top of Billy's house. An alien crept up to Billy while he was asleep.
'It's Christmas.'
'Argh!'

John Murphy (9)
Mablins Lane Primary School, Crewe

The Haunted House

Jim went into the dark haunted house. Bats were hanging, mice were scurrying. Floorboards were squeaking. He searched every room for missing artefacts, searching high and low. By now Jim had got to the attic. He found a skeleton sitting. Suddenly a noise scared Jim. It was thankfully only John.

Alex Banks (10)
Mablins Lane Primary School, Crewe

Untitled

There were 3 girls - Cleo, Emma and Rikki. They went on a boat. Cleo fell into a cave. Rikki and Emma came down. They went into the water and turned into mermaids. They climbed into the boat and went. They had to deal with such a big secret!

Rebecca Leeke (10)
Mablins Lane Primary School, Crewe

Spooks

When I was alone, on my own, I went upstairs but no one was found. Then the telephone rang. I did not answer it. I was scared. When it stopped I heard buzzing. It was Dad mowing the lawn and Mum was trying to tell me it's lunch.

Shane Checkman (10)
Mablins Lane Primary School, Crewe

The Magic Spell

I put in some eyeballs and some cats' whiskers,
I added some tails off puppies. Smelly socks
and itchy wigs added themselves to the pot,
when am I going to stop? Pens and pencils
and paper too, books and frogs, into the stew!
Oops, smoke! What am I to do?

Emily Bell (10)
Mablins Lane Primary School, Crewe

The Worst Day Of My Life

It was big, it was wet. I took my first step, then pulled my leg out again, I was still alive but the cold was biting my flesh away. Someone pushed me in, *help, help!* Everyone stared at me and I was banned from the swimming baths for a year.

Rebekah-Jayne Bradley (10)
Mablins Lane Primary School, Crewe

Blinding Fear

It's coming closer, the monster, a skull on fire with red eyes, it's only 3ft away now, oh no! *Argh!* He wakes up with sweat all over his face, it was that monster, terrifying heart-stoppingly ugly. Jack was just dreaming. He will always fear the monster for lifo.

Andrew Bennett (10)
Mablins Lane Primary School, Crewe

The Old Ladder

I tried to do it, it wasn't easy. My heart was pumping as fast as a bull. I was sweating like a bucket full of water, halfway and I nearly did it. Going down the old rusty ladder, in the dark, was hard work but then I got there.

Tanya Ross (10)
Mablins Lane Primary School, Crewe

Independence Day

A ship floated over Houston, Texas, and fired its laser. Millions dead in a second. They retreated to the mothership. 'It's going to fire its laser. Run.' *Five, four, three, two, one.*
'Oh this game is totally bogus - first to 3.'
Tommy, 'Totally!'
Edward, 'You're on.'
Tommy, 'Yeah, yeah!'

Ryan Brogan (10)
Mablins Lane Primary School, Crewe

The Private Johnson

The siren sounded as the Germans invaded. The constant bombarding spread along the border. The Americans fought back with tactics. The Germans fought back with firepower. The Americans had a special weapon - Johnson, he was a private but very wise. Johnson fired. It's over now but not the darn war.

Charles Pointon (10)
Mablins Lane Primary School, Crewe

The Lazy Girl

I was sitting in my living room and someone knocked at the door, I was too tired to go and answer it so my mum answered it instead. The next day I woke up and noticed that my dad had been sleeping downstairs with the dog Bossy, she's mine, yeah.

Chloe Tomkinson (9)
Mablins Lane Primary School, Crewe

Supernatural

Sam and Dean summoned a demon and made a deal. Sam only had one year to live and then the demon would take him to Hell. One hour before the demon took Sam, he set a trap and put salt all around the house and destroyed him. Sam survived forever.

James Owen (10)
Mablins Lane Primary School, Crewe

Fire

Red Arrows flying. F15 Eagles bombing. Soldiers dying but one survived - Stan was the best soldier, his friend Kenny beside him. The Germans were indestructible - they were killing everyone. They even killed Kenny. I had one life left and one bullet. I fired it. Game over, I was dead.

Adam Bartlem (10)
Mablins Lane Primary School, Crewe

A Nasty Bite

Victoria Tudor had style, fame and all the boys in class! She was so posh that a girl called Tracey Parker was jealous! Unfortunately she got shouted at for saying mean things about Victoria, she got sent to the head teacher, so Tracey bought a viper, it bit Victoria! Ouch!

Katie Brown (9)
Mablins Lane Primary School, Crewe

Death Of An Alien

An alien landed in Lilee's living room. He ran downstairs and started running away from her. When he stopped and paused for breath, she hit him with a book and suddenly he died! She hid his body in the bin and no one ever found out. Novor overl

Amy Billington (10)
Mablins Lane Primary School, Crewe

Untitled

I walked through the doors, loving the smell of roses surrounding me and lavender and the different coloured shapes in every colour and the smiles on everybody's faces with their crisp white clothes. Loads of people are looking, especially at the pink Paris one. Oh … I love the perfume shop.

Lucy King
Mablins Lane Primary School, Crewe

Untitled

I'm petrified. I'm sitting pinned onto my chair and sitting stock-still. There are people all around me. Behind the closed door is the scariest thing ever known to man. Somebody goes through the door. I can hear them screaming.
'Calm down silly!' says Mum laughing, 'it's only the dentist!'

Gemma Warrington (10)
Mablins Lane Primary School, Crewe

Untitled

In the night I could not get to sleep. I think I am blind but how could I be crying trying to get the door handle? I can't see. I was sitting in my bed crying, wondering what had happened. Now I opened my eyes. It was only a dream.

Ashleigh Clarke
Mablins Lane Primary School, Crewe

Untitled

It was dark - my mum and dad put a blindfold on me. They took me to a room. When they took the blindfold off me the room was black. The lights came on and everyone jumped up and said, 'Happy birthday!'
I loved it - it was the best birthday ever.

Chloe Holland
Mablins Lane Primary School, Crewe

The Ghoul School

One ordinary day I went to school. The door sounded creaky, the school was grey. I stepped in. The people were zombies, the teacher looked ugly! My classmates were zombies. I survived. I went home. Mum was a zombie, she killed me and that was the end of my life.

Keegan Bamford (9)
Mablins Lane Primary School, Crewe

Untitled

My throat was tightening, sweat crept down my back. My face went red. My hair stuck up. My legs shook and trembled. There was nobody to help. My cheeks went yellow, my stomach churned. My legs gave way. *Boom!* We stopped. The doors opened. Why was I scared of lifts?

Matthew Minshull
Mablins Lane Primary School, Crewe

Untitled

I was happy. Suddenly the door burst open. The robber tied me up, I was helpless. The rope came loose and I ran to the phone and called 999 but it was broken. I looked around but he was gone and had stolen everything in the living room. No!

Josh Long
Mablins Lane Primary School, Crewe

The Dark Knight

A dragon flew towards the knight with a spear in his hand which slashed the dragon's arm right off, but it grew back. It had a new metal arm now. Now it would have killed the knight if he did not have the pitch-black shield he was still holding

Calum Dutton (10)
Mablins Lane Primary School, Crewe

The End

My head was hurting. My pen was falling out of my grip. I didn't dare move. It was quiet. I was sweaty. *Tick-tock, tick-tock, tick-tock, tick-tock.* Five, four, three, two, one, the end of school, yeah! I could go home and watch TV all night. Yeah!

Thomas Oldham (10)
Mablins Lane Primary School, Crewe

Surprise Party

I sat down and turned on my TV, there was a sudden noise upstairs, I left on my TV and checked all the rooms, nothing was there. I walked down, down the stairs and then there was a surprise. I said, 'Wow, what a lovely birthday party, thank you!'

Stacey Herring (10)
Mablins Lane Primary School, Crewe

Scary Night

My parents went out for the night, I was home alone. I heard a knock at the door, the shape at the door was a funny shape, it scared me. All of a sudden the door burst open. It was my parents, it gave me a fright.
'Are you OK?'

Lauren Griffin (9)
Mablins Lane Primary School, Crewe

The Bad Night

One night at ten to nine I was on my bike near a big, dark, mysterious forest. It was getting creepy. I saw a man with a face of thunder, he was a zombie! He started to chase me! I got on my bike and went home. I told Mum.

Robbie Handley
Mablins Lane Primary School, Crewe

Are We There Yet?

'Are we there yet?' I shouted.
'No we're not,' said my daddy.
'I need the toilet so hurry up.'
'I've forgotten my teddy,' I wailed.
'We are not going back home Bennjy,' said Daddy.
Five minutes later. 'Are we there yet?'
'Yes, nursery is only around the corner,' said Daddy.

Anna Harrison (10)
Mablins Lane Primary School, Crewe

Untitled

Something hairy scary in my room. Oh no, what was that? A scream of terror coming from behind my door. I cuddled in bed. I felt a breezy draft. My head was throbbing with fear, sadness and fright. Then suddenly I woke up at 6am from the nightmare of Hell.

Rebecca Boyd
Mablins Lane Primary School, Crewe

Outer Space

I'm in a spaceship and I am on my ship alone but the jet has come off and I am heading straight to the moon. I'm going to die. I close my eyes and when I open them I am in my bed. Mum has opened the curtains.

George Blythe (10)
Mablins Lane Primary School, Crewe

Funfair

I woke early, I was going to a fair. When I arrived I went straight to the ghost train. The ride was scary but fun, I closed my eyes hoping it would end quickly, it did, but when I opened my eyes I'd been dreaming, I was still in bed.

Lucy Greenall (9)
Monton Green Primary School, Eccles

Rapunzel

A long time ago there was a girl called Rapunzel who lived in a castle. A wicked witch put her there. One day a handsome prince came to rescue her. Beautiful Rapunzel was really excited. While the witch was away the prince rescued her.

Rebecca Dooley (9)
Monton Green Primary School, Eccles

Untitled

Little wolf trotted along to Grandma's where the woodcutter had disguised himself and locked up Grandma.

'What little eyes you've got!' said Wolfy curiously.

Suddenly the woodcutter leapt out of bed slavering hungrily. Just then Hood arrived waving an axe.

'Not you again!' said the woodcutter escaping into the woods.

Jessica Sweeney (9)
Monton Green Primary School, Eccles

The Catch

There I was, ready to throw the ball, I threw the ball, the batter hit the ball, it went up into the air. I caught the ball and I shouted, 'Out!' with excitement. My team came running to me. We won the game. The crowd were overjoyed!

Rebecca Hill (9)
Monton Green Primary School, Eccles

Hide-And-Seek

Lauren ran towards the big old tree at the bottom of the garden. She crouched down behind the thick trunk. Quiet and still she waited. Suddenly, 'Found you!' shouted Joe. Lauren screamed, 'You made me jump.'
They both laughed.
'Your turn,' caid Joe.
Lauren began to count, '1, 2, 3 … '

Lauren Willetts (9)
Monton Green Primary School, Eccles

The Show Must Go On

Backstage my heart was pounding, I could hear the audience whispering with friends and family. The lights went down. Suddenly the music started, we danced on stage, the lights dazzled my eyes. It was amazing. The audience began to applaud. I wanted to do it again and again.

Paige Royle (9)
Monton Green Primary School, Eccles

The Hare And The Tortoise

Once there was a hare and a tortoise. The hare wanted a race with the tortoise, so the tortoise did it. The hare raced ahead and had a nap and the tortoise pulled ahead of the hare and won the race. The hare was so disappeared with himself.

Daniel Wilson (9)
Monton Green Primary School, Eccles

A Trip To The Moon

I woke up and saw a phoenix at my window, he was golden like the sun. 'Do you want to fly to the moon?' he said. I nodded. I jumped on his back and we flew into the sky. We travelled around the moon and was back for breakfast.

Kallen Chapman (9)
Monton Green Primary School, Eccles

It

It slithered, slimed and scraped across the dank, squelching ground. It lurched, I screamed, twisted, stumbled, gasped and thrust. It roared and tumbled. *Thud!* It gasped and shuddered its last breath. I sighed and reached for her hand, guided her out of the darkness and stepped back out into light.

Lydia Power
Our Lady of Pity RC Primary School, Greasby

A Dream Game

This was the highlight of my life. Today, 20 years ago, I was playing for Man United. Besty puts a brilliant cross in to Dennis Law. Dennis puts a cross right across the six yard box, I shoot for the FA Cup.
'Jack, wake up,' shouted Mam. What a dream!

Jack Forster (11)
Plumpton Primary School, Penrith

Boom!

'Die, die evil alien scum! Eat laser you fiends, aha! I am on a roll! Whoa! The mighty skuba! He is no match for my weapons and my skill! He will grovel before me! He will … '
I was blasted off my feet. I lay still, too still. I didn't move.

Richard Sykes (11)
Plumpton Primary School, Penrith

Doomed

Nowhere to run, nowhere to hide, they had me trapped. They snarled constantly, howling into the pitch-black sky. In the blink of an eye one leapt at me. I fired. It fell to the ground stone dead. A second one jumped. I raised my gun but it wouldn't fire …

Harry Hogarth (10)
Plumpton Primary School, Penrith

The Worst Day Ever

One day Louise went out on her horse Spark. The day before that Louise had fallen out with her friends whilst they were on a trek. Suddenly Spark galloped off. Her heart thumped like mad. *Argh!* She fell …

Samantha Bell (9)
Plumpton Primary School, Penrith

Pink

A long time ago in a brightly coloured forest there was a boy lost and hungry. He was looking for food when all of a sudden a pink horse appeared and said, 'Follow me. I will help you with your food, clothes and all your other needs, I have friends.'

Natasha Burns (8)
Portland Primary School, Birkenhead

We're Going On A Slaughter Holiday

A spaceship disembarked on Earth. People widened their eyes in horror and surrounded the metal blue ship. An invasion had begun. 'Everyone will be slaughtered, a terrible bloodbath,' someone screamed.
An alien family stepped out. One of them laughed really loudly. 'We are only on vacation, come on kids.'

Thomas Healey (10)
St Alban's Catholic Primary School, Macclesfield

The Age Of The Dinosaur

Deeper and deeper I fell down the black, whirling hole. I heard a loud roar. Louder and louder it came. *Thump! Bang!* I had fallen to the ground. I looked at the floor, there was something behind me. I turned my head stiffly. There it was. It was a dinosaur.

Emily Wardle (11)
St Alban's Catholic Primary School, Macclesfield

The Death Of The Dinosaurs

There were gigantic fearless dinosaurs. They were eating sweet, pleasant grass. There was something coming down from the bright starlit sky. It was a huge meteorite about the size of a considerable city. The fire was blistering. Dinosaurs started stampoding away. It came with a large bang. Dinosaurs extinct forever.

Tom Ridings (10)
St Alban's Catholic Primary School, Macclesfield

What Could It Be?

A green scaly creature stood on the patio. His protruding eyes looked around. What could it be? It felt the different objects that were in the garden. Slowly the alien trudged through the long green grass. It placed its hand on the door handle and pushed down. Alice was doomed.

Megan Quigley (10)
St Alban's Catholic Primary School, Macclesfield

The Black Mistake

Jim and Ben went looking for gold. One stepped on a huge rock. The steep tunnel closed behind them. Then Ben slipped and went rolling back. He yelled. Jim did not go back to help. It was dim and there were black shadows. Unsafe, he was gazing into the case.

Andrew Loxham (11)
St Alban's Catholic Primary School, Macclesfield

Travelling Spell

She was there, she knew it. She knew that if she didn't do the ancient spell she would never see her parents again. She added the ingredients, said the magic words. Then *boom!* A pink puff of smoke emerged from the pot. She was still at Middlewick Girls' Boarding School.

Hannah Brennan
St Alban's Catholic Primary School, Macclesfield

Little Red

In a dark, dark wood Red swiftly ran to her nanna's house to deliver sweet-smelling, delicious food. Red met a scary, huge wolf and carried on running. When she reached her nanna's house the wolf was there. A strong woodcutter came crashing in from the window to rescue them.

Anna Mattock (11)
St Alban's Catholic Primary School, Macclesfield

Cinderella

Glittering with pride, Cinderella hopped into the golden carriage. Everything was turning out perfectly until clumsy Godmother waved her magic wand and turned Cinderella into an ugly looking witch.

'I can't go to the ball like this. My prince is waiting,' Cinderella sobbed.

'Tough, no one cares, you're ugly anyway!'

Megan Clowes (11)
St Alban's Catholic Primary School, Macclesfield

The Hostage Killer

He jumped into the clean pool, his head vanished, he had sunk. Blood appeared.
'Argh!' yelled Sarah.
Quickly Sarah charged up to the room, screaming as she was grabbed and yanked down. Gore leaked across the floor as the man appeared in a bloodstained suit also holding a bloody knife.

Jake Taylor (11)
St Alban's Catholic Primary School, Macclesfield

Boo!

He lay silently concentrating on the noise. Tiptoeing up the spiral staircase he locked the bedroom door and climbed into bed. He couldn't sleep - squeaking stairs, a thunderous roar. Suddenly the old door opened, who was it?
'I'm home,' shouted Mum entering the room. 'Terrible weather out there isn't it?'

Rachael Perkins (11)
St Alban's Catholic Primary School, Macclesfield

Turn To Dust!

'Turn to dust!' shouted Peter, pointing a wand at his rubber. Rumbling sounds drew near, the earth started shaking and Peter's feet rooted into the ground. Shocked, he realised the spell had failed. He was trapped! Suddenly, light glowed and he heard a bell ringing. He was late for class!

László Zörényi (11)
St Alban's Catholic Primary School, Macclesfield

Captured?

John stared into the murky, shadowed sky. He spotted flashing scarlet lights gleaming. *Strange*, thought John. He examined a circular ship. John crept forward. A green hand touched him, covering him in smoke. A cough, then darkness. Slowly John's eyes opened. Earth was in the distance. The world gone? Forever?

Kevin Wright (11)
St Alban's Catholic Primary School, Macclesfield

The Spell Went Out Of Control

He added a few bits to his destructive spell and it was ready. He started to say the magic words, 'Hip, hop, work well, for this will be my best spell.'

It worked but then he realised it was a big mistake. The ground started to shake. Smoke, then *boom!*

Christopher Weetman (11)
St Alban's Catholic Primary School, Macclesfield

Eruption

We stared into the volcano.
'Of course this volcano has been dormant for centuries,' droned our guide. Smoke rose like a serpent from the crater. 'This happens all the time,' stuttered the guide. Suddenly a *boom!* Rocks, falling! Ash, rising! I ran.
Later I emerged from my hiding place. Alone.

Rachel Horner (11)
St Alban's Catholic Primary School, Macclesfield

World War 3

It came in a flash of blue lights, scorching my garden. A ship! The alien fell out, injured. 'You'll be fine,' I whispered.
Days later the alien had grown huge and powerful. 'I must feast,' it said, ripping out my guts. Darkness. Forgotten secrets would be revealed in the invasion.

Nicholas Phillips (10)
St Alban's Catholic Primary School, Macclesfield

Another Victim

The tyrannosaurus lunged at the triceratops, its huge teeth sliced into the triceratop's flesh. Blood poured from the dinosaur as it began to collapse. The tyrannosaurus had eliminated yet another victim from its path. It ripped flesh from bone, just leaving the carcass of the triceratops on the sandy plains.

Jonathan Thompson (10)
St Alban's Catholic Primary School, Macclesfield

Crazy Door

Reaching for the rusty door handle Lucy breathed slowly. She twisted it, there was a sudden noise. *Creak!* Pink grass, green sky, candy-covered houses, Lucy had opened the door into a magical world. Puzzled, her eyes were glued to this peculiar place. Yep, she was definitely in Planet Crazy!

Lauren Smethurst (11)
St Alban's Catholic Primary School, Macclesfield

Alien Invasion

The alien zapped the humans. If bullets couldn't stop it what could?
'Get me your leader!'
'We don't have a leader,' said a soldier.
'You do now!'
The evil alien picked off every human like petals from a flower. The world was taken over. Game over, the PS2 turned off.

Aidan Smith (11)
St Alban's Catholic Primary School, Macclesfield

The Travellers

We are the travellers. We have travelled through time and space, never stopping at any single planet. We travelled to the future and decided to stop. Annoyingly our touring invention was destroyed. Stuck there for all eternity on a lonely hot desert where no animals dared to come on, ever.

Arran McCloskey (11)
St Alban's Catholic Primary School, Macclesfield

Trapped!

John awoke lying in the corner of a damp, dark cave. To his disappointment the man was slouching in a chair, fast asleep. Time was tick-tocking away and the man awoke. The kidnapper sprang to his feet. *Bang!* John felt his pulse and encountered a snake curled up, dead.

Robert Nowak (11)
St Alban's Catholic Primary School, Macclesfield

Oh No!

'Hocus pocus, zippy zap.'
'I can't believe it.'
Thomas had become even smaller, he was now thirty centimetres. Merlin apologised. Merlin put a frog, eye of newt and acid into the slimy concoction. Tom drank the potion, he shrunk to a tiny two inches.
'Oh no not again,' he cried.

Callum Byrne (11)
St Alban's Catholic Primary School, Macclesfield

Surprise!

Fred couldn't sleep because it was his birthday. He tiptoed downstairs trying not to wake anyone. Hearing a noise from his garden he ran to see what it was. His eyes swelled, his heart thumped. Aliens cornered him. Fred screamed in horror. *'Help!'* He would die on his birthday

...

Surprise!

Michael Jennings (11)
St Alban's Catholic Primary School, Macclesfield

Jack's Death

Jack sprinted to the busy old supermarket. His mother made him sell the heavy, smelly cow. Then a poor, silent man quickly came with magic beans. His mother charged at him. Jack sped up the beanstalk whilst the giant rushed at him. Jack hurtled to the ground like a stone.

Mark Elkommos (11)
St Alban's Catholic Primary School, Macclesfield

Boom!

The huge silver spaceship landed at Manchester Airport. An alien which had a large head and was green appeared out of it. The creature grabbed some eyeballs to pay the taxi driver. 'Green Man Inn please.' The alien had two beers, two Cokes, a lemonade, before his gigantic head exploded.

Jack Pritchard (11)
St Alban's Catholic Primary School, Macclesfield

The Ghost Of Your Past

Isabel positioned the glistening necklace around her neck. It was shaped like a heart. She felt sleepy and climbed into bed. Suddenly she heard a voice. 'I am the ghost of your past and I will bring back all your bad memories.' Distraught, she threw the necklace out the window.

Anna Harrington (11)
St Alban's Catholic Primary School, Macclesfield

An Expected Visit

When Tom woke up he spotted a green, giant, four-eyed alien in his room. Tom was worried it would eat him. The monster took his tentacle out and was going to strangle Tom. Tom dodged quickly. Tom put his hand around the three-legged alien's neck and killed him.

Jake Turner (10)
St Alban's Catholic Primary School, Macclesfield

The Assassination Process

Blue and green lights flashed on the metallic ship. A ramp descended from the UFO, a foot appeared, followed by a body. Extendable claws flashed, serrated teeth bared. It stepped out and growled, 'Give us David Beckham, he must go through assassination process!' Only screams filled the ship that night.

Thomas Kaye (11)
St Alban's Catholic Primary School, Macclesfield

Enchantment

Warlock Mungo was sitting in his tower finishing the difficult spell. 'Ekhanum, enchantum!' he chanted. He stopped. He misread the spell, the amulet was enchanted but at what cost? Fire consumed the tower. Singed, he rubbed the amulet again. Millions of demons appeared. 'Now the fun begins,' he smiled. 'Attack!'

Matthew McFahn (11)
St Alban's Catholic Primary School, Macclesfield

The Assassin

The assassin had been on the run for two long years now. He was about to make his next kill. He pulled out his gun and shot. The cream-carpeted floor was covered in sticky red blood. With the dead body lying on the floor the assassin made his escape.

Thomas Priest (10)
St Alban's Catholic Primary School, Macclesfield

The Eagle Who Thought He Knew Everything

There was once an eagle who thought he knew everything. Everyone believed him except Mr Sparrow, the school teacher.
One day, Mr Sparrow saw the eagle secretly looking at the book in class. At once he stopped class, ran outside and proved to everyone that the eagle didn't know everything.

Sarah Hooper (8)
St Bega's CE Primary School, Holmrook

Questions You Can Never Ask

Oh, it's disgusting. It's green, don't look, stay away. It sits at the back of the class picking its toenails, eating green goo and oh you don't want to know! Is it a girl? Is it a boy? Nobody knows. What is It? How is it? I don't know!

Abigail Cookman (10)
St Bega's CE Primary School, Holmrook

Humpty Dumpty

There was an egg wobbling on a wall. Everyone shouted, 'No!' but it was too late. Scrambled egg covered the floor. All the King's horses and all the King's men waded in and stuck him back together. They put him back on the wall, where he wobbled like scrambled jelly.

Emily Tyson (10)
St Bega's CE Primary School, Holmrook

Monster

It lives in your room, under your bed. It is green and slimy. It makes your room a mess. It only comes out at night-time. It makes you scared. All it eats is boys. I play with mine. Do not be worried. All it is is very bad, beware!

Emma Thornley (9)
St Bega's CE Primary School, Holmrook

Jack And Jill

There once was a brother and sister called Jack and Jill. One day their mother asked them to go and get a bucket of water from the well at the top of the hill. So they set off up the hill. Jack fell in the well because Jill pushed him.

Jessica Harrison
St Bega's CE Primary School, Holmrook

Run For My Life

I ran, faster than the wind! My feet pounded the hard ground! My hands were trembling with fear! Was he behind me, following me? No! I felt isolated, on my own! I was lost in the huge forest! Suddenly, wide open hands grabbed me. I stared in horror! I screamed!

Emma Riley (9)
St Gilbert's RC Primary School, Eccles

The King Of Wolves

One harsh winter night, the king of wolves proudly sat upon the edge of the rough ice-cold cliff, when the bloodthirsty bats attacked him. The king of wolves dodged, snapped and tossed them. When the battle was over he saw his body cut, bleeding and dead.

Liam McCusker (9)
St Gilbert's RC Primary School, Eccles

Lily And The Dreaded Ballet Exam

Sometimes Lily doesn't like things, although she loves dancing. When dancing Lily's as graceful as a bird. She had a ballet exam coming up and she was really nervous. She didn't expect it to be so nerve-racking. Her fists were clenched, oh my goodness! She walked in the door …

Amy Ruddle (9)
St Gilbert's RC Primary School, Eccles

Boom!

A boy named Bob was sent to bed by his father. It was only 6.55pm. He waddled up the stairs. He changed into his pyjamas. He dived into bed. 5 minutes later … *boom!* Bob looked under his bed. Mr Dino had lost a leg and an eye. He'd come alive!

Tom Mosey (9)
St Gilbert's RC Primary School, Eccles

Broken

One summer's day I embarked on a ride that had eight loops. It stopped on the first one upside down. Then I tumbled out of the cart and I went down a hole. 'Argh!'

Charlotte Stoddard (9)
St Gilbert's RC Primary School, Eccles

When I Saw The Alien

On one normal day, I was just doing the washing up and then it just landed in my back garden. A huge, beaming cylinder spaceship in my back garden. Then a glowing, slithering alien came out, looked around for something then stopped. Then he took my dad's T-shirt.

Sarah Garratt (9)
St Gilbert's RC Primary School, Eccles

Untitled

Eyes watering, she's crossing her fingers, biting her tongue and toes clenched. She's so excited. So am I. Mum and Dad are going to a meeting, we have the whole house to ourselves. Yes! We are going to sneak out and go on the terrifying Traumerizer, here goes! Argh!

Emily Devine (9)
St Gilbert's RC Primary School, Eccles

The Alien

Hands clammy, body tense, eyes focused, teeth clenched. I'm staring at the alien and it's staring back. I think I'm going to make it. Argh! Yahoo, I got it, no more Angelina Ballerina, it's time for Monster Truck Rally. My sister's never gonna get her hands on the remote again.

Erin Clemans (9)
St Gilbert's RC Primary School, Eccles

Untitled

One day a green slimy alien stepped out of his ship. He was tall. He mumbled to himself. He was a jumpy little alien. He saw humans. He went mad. He threw stuff like spoons and rocks. He suddenly got back in his ship and disappeared.

Alex Rogers (9)
St Gilbert's RC Primary School, Eccles

Untitled

Once I came home from school, there stood a fat red-eyed alien. I stood with my fists crunched, eyes blinking. The alien chased me around the house. Then with his eyes he froze me. I never moved again.

Ruby Howard (9)
St Gilbert's RC Primary School, Eccles

A Wedding Trip

I am going to a wedding on a train. I have been excited all year. I am getting on the train. I start going. I have been onboard for two hours now. Suddenly the train stops in the middle of nowhere. I am lost, I don't know what to do.

Molly Glynn-Whitehead (9)
St Gilbert's RC Primary School, Eccles

Christmas Day

On Christmas Day a wacky, cheeky mini girl called Phoebe came down the stairs with butterflies in her stomach. She went into the garden and saw an adorable miniature Shetland which was called Buttons. She said, 'He is absolutely gorgeous.' She also said, 'It is amazing to have a pony!'

Eleanor Dean (8)
St Gilbert's RC Primary School, Eccles

The Mysterious Man

One cold, frosty night a naughty, skinny, young boy was throwing snowballs over a fence. He saw a mysterious man with a cloak on. He aggressively opened the door of his house. The boy tried to open his door. It just opened enough to get in there. No one there!

George Hughes (9)
St Gilbert's RC Primary School, Eccles

The Scary Humpty Dumpty

Humpty Dumpty tumbles off the ginormous wall, he's unconscious. He has a terrible dream, he has cast a spell on a little boy. The boy has turned into a pig. Humpty Dumpty tries to turn him back. He turns him into a whale. Humpty wakes up, he is a whale!

Leah Glynn (9)
St Gilbert's RC Primary School, Eccles

I've Found A Pixie!

I was strolling down the rocky road and I saw movement in the bush. I strolled over and picked up something light. It was a pixie! I hid it under my bed. Later I found the pixie … ill. I decided to let it go. I waved until my arm ached.

Lucy O'Reilly (8)
St Gilbert's RC Primary School, Eccles

The Egg Head

One day Humpty Dumpty went for a stroll. He walked to the local kitchen to go on beds. He glimpsed at a strange looking bed up high so he tried it out. Humpty felt a strange heat coming from underneath him. Then the scrambling began. *Argh! Please help!*

Tom Nuttall (9)
St Gilbert's RC Primary School, Eccles

Dropping

I screamed as I dropped, I wished I was somewhere else, anywhere but not here. I closed my eyes and counted to 10, it wasn't over. I straightened out hoping it would go faster. I finally plunged into the pool with a splash. Why do I hate diving boards?

Rachel Kenyon (11)
St Gregory's Catholic Primary School, Workington

The Yeti

It was freezing. Sweat ran down my back, it felt as if all my courage had gone down a dark hole and all that was left was fear. Then I walked on and heard *stomp! Stomp!* and a very loud *roar!* I fell to the floor and fainted.

Daniel Robinson (11)
St Gregory's Catholic Primary School, Workington

Princess And The Frog

A frog went to kiss a princess. He put out his lips but Princess refused, got under her covers and stayed there until the frog moved. The frog crept on her bed and cried. The princess felt hard-hearted and kissed him. He turned to a prince, they lived happily.

Jaye Poland (10)
St Gregory's Catholic Primary School, Workington

The Silly Wizard

He went down the old crooked stairs, hoping his potion would work. All of a sudden, *bang!* the potion went wrong. He suddenly fell to the floor with a puff. He was gone. No one knew where he was and that was the end of his potion life.

Amelia-Jane Gregory (11)
St Gregory's Catholic Primary School, Workington

The Deadly Flight

'Careful,' said Daren. He was flying the plane from Hawaii. It all started when somebody loaded the plane with 150 poisonous venom snakes. The snakes attacked and killed. The only evidence anybody ever found was 24 dead bodies and a crashed plane. Those horrible creatures feasted on those poor souls.

Lindsey Kelly (10)
St Gregory's Catholic Primary School, Workington

Help!

I heard a loud bang, then suddenly the warning siren went off. *Oh no, it's a bomb!* I thought. I jumped off the settee, scurrying quickly to the Anderson shelter. I pounced into the shelter. I was safe. All I could hear was the loud bangs outside the shelter.

Sarah Robertson (11)
St Gregory's Catholic Primary School, Workington

The Fast And The Furious

Brian was in the Tokyo Drift Race when he heard the roar of the engine and then *vroom!* They all zoomed off, the smell of burning rubber filled the air with a deadly gas, then suddenly Brian flicked a switch, went the speed of lightning and then blew up.

Niall Bainbridge (10)
St Gregory's Catholic Primary School, Workington

The Mermaid

The mermaid flew through the air, then went splosh back into the sea. She dived down to the sea bottom for she had found an oyster shell. She cracked it open. Her eyes gleamed, for in the shell there lay a pearl. She smiled at the beautiful treasure before her.

Rachel Carter (11)
St Gregory's Catholic Primary School, Workington

The Dolphin

The dolphin was swimming in the sea, then the dolphin flew through the air and went slowly down back into the sea. It made a huge splash. It swam to the bottom of the sea and found a piece of gold. It looked puzzled and didn't know what to do.

Chelsia Austin (11)
St Gregory's Catholic Primary School, Workington

King Cobra

The giant king cobra ripped the tops of buildings off and spat poison so that the people would burn in pain. It slithered and wreaked havoc everywhere it went. A tank aimed its rocket and locked it on. The tank fired the rocket. *Bang!* It hit the snake, dead.

Ryan Allenby (11)
St Gregory's Catholic Primary School, Workington

The Thing!

I walked into my room. Suddenly it was on the wall. I stood still like a statue. I slowly opened the door. I crept down my stairs. Another one was on my fireplace. My heart was beating fast. I walked outside. I couldn't believe it … Argh! I don't like spiders!

James Simpson (11)
St Laurence's Catholic Primary School, Liverpool

Best Friends

It was Saturday, my best friend's birthday. I felt a bit sick. I ran to the bathroom as fast as I could. I had to ring my friend up. I felt like a bully. She was upset the next day. My mum said, 'We could go for a meal.'

Emmi Gee (11)
St Laurence's Catholic Primary School, Liverpool

Lost In The Woods

I was walking along the woods on a dark evening. I walked along the large bushy trees. It went dark. I couldn't see, I could only hear noises. It felt like someone was following me. I ran but tripped. As I got up I could see huge foot in front

Antonia Gorman (11)
St Laurence's Catholic Primary School, Liverpool

Buried

The air is so cold, it feels like I'm in the water already - *splash!* Quivering all over even down to my fingertips, I bop up. The air is gloomy, this triangle is a mystery. And just minutes ago I was on a plane, now pulled down … I'm sunk forever.

Chloe Atherton (11)
St Laurence's Catholic Primary School, Liverpool

A Fairy Tale - The Fly

I got up for a drink. I thought I'd seen a fairy. I went into my bedroom. I was closing the door, when … I heard something. I got in my bed and closed my eyes. I heard that noise again. So I got up, I saw it, 'It's a fly!'

Dominic Castell (11)
St Laurence's Catholic Primary School, Liverpool

A Trip To The Shop

Tracey went to the shops with her mum to see what she wanted for her birthday. That was it … right there in front of her was a brand new scooter that was just out. Tracey asked her mum and she said, 'Maybe.'
It was her birthday, Tracey got the scooter.

Megan Egan (11)
St Laurence's Catholic Primary School, Liverpool

The Swimming Baths

As I opened the door I walked on a slippery floor. I looked around and saw lots of monsters on little boats. I ran around the side on the wet floor. Then, a spooky man on a ladder shouted, 'Stop running!' Then I remembered, I was at the swimming baths.

Adam Campbell (11)
St Laurence's Catholic Primary School, Liverpool

Troy And The Monster

Troy collapsed against the palace walls. He shut his eyes and prayed. His prayer wasn't answered. He could hear the repulsive monster's feet thumping on the ground. Suddenly, he grabbed his razor-sharp blade, stabbing the hideous monster in the leg. The monster crashed in the burning fire, killing him!

Holly Hughes (11)
St Laurence's Catholic Primary School, Liverpool

The House

She ran for the door but it vanished. Footsteps walked the room, there was someone there. She could hear breathing. She turned, there was nobody there. The door appeared, she reached for it, something pulled her back. She lot out a piercing screech … and she was never found!

Shelley Blackburn (11)
St Laurence's Catholic Primary School, Liverpool

Lost And Alone

School had finished. I thought I would take a shortcut home. After a while, I noticed I was walking through strange alleyways I'd never seen before. I couldn't remember where I went wrong. I was lost. Lost and alone!

Jadeine Fagan (11)
St Laurence's Catholic Primary School, Liverpool

The Creature

What's that weird green thing opening the door?
Kay thought. She looked terrified, it looked evil and frightening. Kay pulled the covers over her head, she could hear the creature whispering to her … 'Get out of bed, get out of bed!'
She looked at the creature .. 'Oh Dad, it's you!'

Kay Bell (11)
St Laurence's Catholic Primary School, Liverpool

The Creature

She looked around, there were two walls either side of her and they seemed to stretch onwards. Suddenly, something scampered across her feet. She jumped and followed it. She had lost sight of the creature and kept on running forward. She fainted. The creature was her little black cat, Cole.

Samantha Nairn (11)
St Laurence's Catholic Primary School, Liverpool

The Battle Of Olympus

Zeus was all alone. Then suddenly Hades appeared in a puff of black smoke. 'I'm here to take over Olympus big brother and you can't stop me!' screamed Hades.

Zeus just laughed. He threw a thunderbolt at Hades. *Zap!* Hades was hit.

'I'll be back!' screamed Hades. Olympus was saved!

Aimeé Halleron (11)
St Laurence's Catholic Primary School, Liverpool

The Black Church

When Ed and Frank walked into the black church, the doors slammed shut. It was pitch-black inside. Then Ed and Frank walked upstairs and climbed onto the pillars. Then suddenly … the pillar shook and Frank fell off. Ed hung on and then, in horror, Frank died.

Paul Richmond (11)
St Laurence's Catholic Primary School, Liverpool

Lost In The Woods

The forest was very quiet. All you could hear were the birds tweeting in the bushy trees. A loud noise came from the scary house. I could hear someone laughing in the distance. I was so frightened I ran out the house to find myself back in the dense woods.

Lauren McArdle (11)
St Laurence's Catholic Primary School, Liverpool

Monster!

It's big, it's green, it creeps me out. It lives in my wardrobe! I lay still at night so it doesn't see me. Sometimes I even think I can hear it moaning. At this point in my life I regret one thing, letting my nan knit me a green sweater.

Kevin Furlong (11)
St Laurence's Catholic Primary School, Liverpool

The Holiday Of Doom

Suzanne sat trembling, staring out of her window as the haze got closer and closer. Her fears were growing stronger. Passengers were biting their nails severely, worrying whether this holiday was worth the distress. Was it just a myth? Obviously not ... everyone was mysteriously disappearing into the Bermuda Triangle's mist.

Sian Bradshaw (11)
St Laurence's Catholic Primary School, Liverpool

The Steam Monsters

I saw fat, hairy monsters in robes. The door was locked, they were surrounding me as the sweat dripped off their bushy hair onto the floor. The monsters were pouring water into a pan, to make the room even hotter, but I realised it was the sauna room.

Ben Dillon (11)
St Laurence's Catholic Primary School, Liverpool

The House

At the end of our street there is the most unusual house I've ever seen. No one has lived in it for twenty years. Anyone who's gone by it hasn't ever come back. Everyone thinks that there is a lonely ghost who wants to have some company. What do you think?

Jake Lunt (11)
St Laurence's Catholic Primary School, Liverpool

The Rodeo

The rodeo began, sending horses galloping around the track. Becky was spooked! Rearing with her head held high, Emily hitting the ground with an almighty thump. Silence … I rushed over, screaming for help! I ran and stopped Becky from rearing - was this the end of Emily and her dream adventure?

Emily Canning (11)
St Laurence's Catholic Primary School, Liverpool

Alice And The Tomb

Alice was standing outside the entrance, her parents allowed her to go in. Alice entered the tomb, she wished she hadn't … it had closed up, she was imprisoned as she tried to find an exit. Mummies were attacking her - but it was just her mum shaking her to wake up!

Aidan Watkinson (11)
St Laurence's Catholic Primary School, Liverpool

The Fright!

It was dark in the field. When suddenly, a light burst from over the trees. I couldn't see anything. I thought for a moment, then went to investigate. It's a UFO. I walked in and saw something green, it came towards me and shouted, 'Boo!' It was my annoying dad!

Callum Conning (11)
St Laurence's Catholic Primary School, Liverpool

Surprise Around The Corner

I skipped home after school, I shouted, 'Mum?' I was going to Chloe's house but no one answered. This was starting to scare me. I ran to Chloe's house and told her to come home with me. We went to the door and kicked it open. Suddenly everyone shouted …
'Surprise!'

Laura Brown (11)
St Laurence's Catholic Primary School, Liverpool

The Trip!

I was playing on the riverbank when I slipped. I had fallen in the lake. I couldn't swim. I thought I was going to die! I tried to move, my body was frozen with fright! I screamed, no one heard me. A passer-by heard my cries, I was saved!

Stephanie Stuart (11)
St Laurence's Catholic Primary School, Liverpool

Troy And The Minotaur

Troy was left alone with his eyes set on the Minotaur. There was no turning back. A boulder fell, hitting the Minotaur - it was awakened. Troy withdrew his blade, he was ready for battle. The Minotaur charged in. Troy suddenly side-stepped the beast, the Minotaur fell down the cliff.

Bradley O'Connor (11)
St Laurence's Catholic Primary School, Liverpool

Who Was It?

It was a black starless night. I was looking through the window with Alice, seeing embarrassing Edna sizzling because of the hot chilli sauce we put in her cup of tea! 'She's boiling over!' I giggled. Alice giggled too. Suddenly the lights went off in Edna's room. 'Argh!' screamed Edna!

Keeley Porter (11)
St Laurence's Catholic Primary School, Liverpool

Scary Future

Metal, wires and more metal. I entered this odd building and suddenly everything changed - robots and high technology. Did I teleport to the future? I tried to escape, but robots blocked the way. They're making this familiar machine with bright eyes, I read the small label - it clearly said 'BMW'!

Ronce Carl N Saputil (11)
St Luke's RC Primary School, Frodsham

The Fatal Journey

A dwarf gave a girl an apple, she coughed and choked then fell to the floor! Immediately he searched mountains and oceans for a special medicine. The next day he returned, having failed his quest, but the young girl just went, 'Happy April Fool's Day! I'm hungry, what's for dinner?'

Victoria Garner (11)
St Luke's RC Primary School, Frodsham

Princess Ellie

One day Princess Ellie was out horse riding when she tumbled into a polluted pond. When she climbed out a frog had attached himself to her. When she screamed the frog disappeared and was replaced by a voice at the bathroom door.
'Hello! Are you ready yot, Princess?' enquired Dad.

Ellie Ford (11)
St Luke's RC Primary School, Frodsham

Exhausted

My legs are so tired. I feel like I've been walking forever. The pain is getting worse. It's travelling through my whole body. Oh my ankles! I just want to go home and collapse onto my bed.
'Have we done yet?' I whined.
'This is the last shop,' Mum said.

Emma-Louise Pyatt (11)
St Luke's RC Primary School, Frodsham

The Abominable Snowman

I was running around, playing in the snow with my friends when a big whirlwind of snow appeared! A snowman stood right in front of me! He stared at me for a long time, then eventually said, 'HI!' I stood there and screamed. It was my dad! Weird or what?

Lauren Creamer (11)
St Luke's RC Primary School, Frodsham

A Surprising Experience

I could feel my bones click together, and my heart beat faster. I could hear the footsteps coming up the stairs as Mum walked in with the biggest knife from the kitchen.
'Would you like an almond brownie?' she said. 'They're yummy.'
'Well maybe just the one or maybe two.'

Abigail Dimelow (10)
St Luke's RC Primary School, Frodsham

The Monster

Moaning, groaning I heard as I slept in fear. This horrible beast got louder and I got more scared. It said to me, 'I know where you are!' So I tried to find where it was coming from. It was still groaning but it was just my dad, fast asleep!

Faith Howley (11)
St Luke's RC Primary School, Frodsham

The Quest

As I fought my way through scorching deserts, poisonous insects and deadly snakes. Swam through shark-infested waters, stung by many jellyfish and nearly eaten alive by piranhas. As I climbed over rocky mountains, in freezing temperatures with icy winds. Finally, I got there, to find my chocolate was eaten!

Jamie Milne (11)
St Luke's RC Primary School, Frodsham

An Alien Visits Earth

I turned around and standing there was a green, gooey alien! I was extremely frightened. It was strange as it only had one eye and it was very tall. He was a friendly alien but he still scared me! I suddenly woke and realised my brother was in my room!

Emily Mann (11)
St Luke's RC Primary School, Frodsham

The Oblivion

I was trapped! Sitting next to strange things I heard screaming. I looked down and saw utter darkness in a round hole. I hung over an edge and saw gas and metal then I plummeted. Pure nothing was around me, then there was light! My friends won't like this ride!

James Martin (11)
St Luke's RC Primary School, Frodsham

The Journey Round

The world is passing by, I am trembling all over,
my hands are shaking, I need to close my eyes.
Here I am, going round and round. At last my
feet are safely on the ground. I wish I did not
have a fear of going on the London Eye.

Charlotte Read (10)
St Luke's RC Primary School, Frodsham

My Scary Experience

I was trembling all over. My hands were shaking and my heart was thumping loudly. My stomach suddenly turned as I started to fall lower and lower.
'Argh!' At last I could feel my feet safely on the ground. I wish I was not so afraid of travelling down slides.

Charlotte Rose (11)
St Luke's RC Primary School, Frodsham

Bath Time

I ran as fast as I could. I was trembling really badly. I was scared. I hid behind the wardrobe. Somebody was coming. The man picked me up as I screamed, 'Argh! I don't want to go in the bath, it hurts my eyes.'
But Dad said, 'You have to!'

Adam Webb (10)
St Luke's RC Primary School, Frodsham

The Mini Monster

The pink marshmallow rolled towards me. It was nibbling my toe! Was it trying to eat me? My toe had turned pink! What's this? A pair of black, beady eyes seemed to say, 'If you touch me, I bite.' Suddenly, I woke up. Never eat millions of marshmallows before bed!

Caitlin Baxendale (10)
St Philip's CE Primary School, Liverpool

All Alone

I was broken-hearted. My best friend was lying there on a rock. I knelt down beside him and started to cry. A while later I stood up and was on my way. I looked back and my friend was standing there. Then suddenly, I could tell I was safe.

Natalie Baker (10)
St Philip's CE Primary School, Liverpool

Who's There?

It was a pitch-black night. The moon had vanished. Suddenly, *clash!* Was that the gate? I hugged myself with fear … *creak!* Is someone coming up the stairs? Flashbacks of nightmares stalked me! Sweat crept down my back like a hand. I opened the door … it was only my dog!

Lauren Keegan (10)
St Philip's CE Primary School, Liverpool

Being Brave

Silence. No noise. Apart from the distant noise of my sister snoring. I decide to be brave, and get up, but I only end up running back. I am scared of something attacking me. I'll have to go sometime or another. I wish dearly I wasn't so scared of toilets.

Jessica Taylor (9)
St Philip's CE Primary School, Liverpool

Tiny Tales North West England

All Alone!

Completely unaccompanied. 'Mum!' I shout repeatedly. Silence! No answer. I begin to cry. Heart thumping like a big bass drum! *Gulp!* I hear a rattle. The lock clicks! I freeze!
'Hello,' Mum says. I run to hug her. I will have to get used to staying alone in the house!

Amy Perrin (10)
St Philip's CE Primary School, Liverpool

Fear And Fun

Terrified of what might happen. It started and went round the bend and suddenly stopped for a minute then whooshed off but not too fast. It did unexpected things like dips which I didn't know were there. I came off the roller coaster laughing because I'd had so much fun!

Stacey Forrestill (10)
St Philip's CE Primary School, Liverpool

Alton Towers Air!

Trembling upside down. My feet off the ground. I feel like I'm going to fall. I shut my eyes as tight as I can. I get flung everywhere. I try to think of good things but the terrifying thought is there. Will this roller coaster ride ever end? It's fab!

Megan Smith (10)
St Philip's CE Primary School, Liverpool

Whack On The Head!

I ran after my friend in the sunless dusty room. *Whack!* His head hit an endless metal rusty bar. Sitting silently by my lifeless best friend. Then, suddenly, I woke up sweating in my bed. How I wish I did not have nightmares. Sitting up I realise it's a dream.

Craig Collins (10)
St Philip's CE Primary School, Liverpool

My Turn Next!

Waiting. My heart's thumping in my chest like thunder. It's my turn next! I get in the seat with my mum, my cousin and my brother behind me. 5, 4, 3, 2, 1, here we go! It was faster than a motorbike, quicker than a car. Upside down. Loved it!

Amy-Jo Tyrrell (10)
St Philip's CE Primary School, Liverpool

Stuck All Alone!

I am stuck, all alone. All of a sudden the light bursts. I have a phone call off my mobile. It says, 'Where are you?' I sit there in the cold dark corner. Suddenly it starts moving. I have got to get used to lifts - the horrifying lift …

Amy Thomas (10)
St Philip's CE Primary School, Liverpool

Evil Angels

Terrified, in an abandoned basement, surrounded by five murderous stone angels which will send me back in time if I blink, or look away. Suddenly, I blink. The angel appears practically right over me. The angels have long hair, ragged cloaks, and jagged teeth. A flash! They've been tricked.

Neil Seddon (10)
St Philip's CE Primary School, Liverpool

The Dark Room

My spine tingles! Noises, shadows and complete darkness. The light flickers, I look behind me, running shadows! 'Arrggh,' I scream. I look in my dog's bed. He's gone. I run away! 'Buddy,' I call for my dog. He won't come. Another shadow but it's Buddy's shadow. I am so scared!

Liam Morrison (10)
St Philip's CE Primary School, Liverpool

Scream

Nightmares. Scary movies fill my head. Getting chased down a dark scary alleyway by something with a razor-edged pointy knife. Down every street, road, alleyway. But he still hasn't got me. Then I'm caught, woken up in fear, amazed he hasn't got me, it's only a dream.

Brandon Cannell (10)
St Philip's CE Primary School, Liverpool

The Dark Night

Alone in the darkness, I heard a rustling noise. There was something creeping up my bed. It nearly reached my head. Panic! I grabbed my torch, turning it straight away. It was only my cat! He must have snuck in. I wished I wasn't scared of the dark.

Luke Straiton (10)
St Philip's CE Primary School, Liverpool

Tiny Tales North West England

The Strange Noise

I woke up: I heard a strange noise. The curtain moved. The window was open! I shut it. Maybe a monster was in there! Maybe it's outside! Was I dreaming? Maybe it wasn't a monster! I looked around. It was my alarm clock. I wish I'd remembered I'd set it …

Melanie Grandidge (9)
St Stephen's CE Primary School, Banks

Jade And The Taxi

Jade had agreed to visit her cousin. The taxi went the wrong way, stopping in a forest. The driver said, 'Get out.' She was scared stiff and ran for her life. Suddenly there was a loud noice, and she realised it was her alarm clock - it was all a dream.

Anthony Pilcher (9)
St Stephen's CE Primary School, Banks

Visiting Earth

A long time ago many people saw a spaceship crash into a desert. They all went to see what was in it. An alien jumped out on top of them. Thousands of people ran! Then the alien got back in the ship and took off rapidly back home.

Corey Flannery (9)
St Stephen's CE Primary School, Banks

The Evil Stairs

My legs were aching. I nearly broke my leg and neck and nearly cracked my skull. But I'm still alive, which is good for me. And that night I had a bad dream about the evil stairs …

Luke Evans (9)
St Stephen's CE Primary School, Banks

Tom The Mean Cat

Once there was a cat named Tom, he was a very mean cat who liked to chase birds. One day a huge eagle swooped down and tried to pick Tom up but Tom was very scared and he hid behind a tree, he never chased a bird ever again.

Laura Jones (9)
St Stephen's CE Primary School, Banks

The Beast In The Night

My tent was dark and cold. I heard the sound of heavy breathing outside. It was loud and scary. I knew the creature was massive. What should I do, open the flap or shout for help? Opening the flap slightly it was there looking at me. The farmer's cow, Daisy.

Richard Gaskell (9)
St Stephen's CE Primary School, Banks

The Wizard's Magic Spell

One day a wizard tried a spell. He mixed all the ingredients together. There were all sorts of things, frogs' legs, eyeballs and fuzz bombs. After ten minutes the wizard drank the potion and as quick as a flash he turned into a huge, furry, white, cuddly and magic cat.

Bradley Garton (9)
St Stephen's CE Primary School, Banks

The Bear

As I walked into the cave I felt fear and fright run down my spine. As I walked into the darkness I heard a great roar. I stumbled back. I nearly fell to the ground. I saw a big shape run towards me.
'Very good,' shouted my drama teacher.

Ryan Ousey (9)
St Stephen's CE Primary School, Banks

Warriors Ride The Ocean

I was sailing along the ocean with my Viking warriors when suddenly there was a flash of lightning, the ocean lit up. Waves crashed together like white horses. The boat was wildly swaying. Warriors shouted, 'Help!' 'Help!' Frightened and helpless we clung to the ship and each other in fear.

Louis Wright (9)
St Stephen's CE Primary School, Banks

Pulling At My Hand

It grasped my hand. It tugged and tugged, digging into my skin until it began to sting. It got more and more painful. I thought it would never stop. Eventually, the thing dropped to the ground. It moved slightly, then died. I wish it was easier to fly a kite!

Charlotte Smith (9)
St Stephen's CE Primary School, Banks

The Scary Height

My heart was pounding, it seemed like it had been 100 years getting to the top of the ride. Then those 100 years flew by in a matter of seconds as I shot down the Pepsi Max - to the end of the ride.

Cameron Williams (9)
St Stephen's CE Primary School, Banks

The Majestic Alien

One day a jelly majestic wicked alien came in his steel invisible spaceship. He flew to Earth and swallowed everyone in his path. Everyone was running manically all over the place, and when he was full he returned to his mysterious planet and no one was on Earth again.

Joshua Moniz (9)
St Stephen's CE Primary School, Banks

The Magician's Mixed Up Spell

A magician named Marvin was going to perform a spell. Standing on stage, he placed a little white rabbit into a hat. He placed a red spotted handkerchief on top. He said, 'Abra Cadabra,' and removed the spotted handkerchief. There sat the rabbit, but the hat was gone …

Bryony Fitzpatrick (9)
St Stephen's CE Primary School, Banks

The Light

It was Friday night and we were in our tents and saw something glowing in the darkness. It was about to pounce on me. 'Argh!' I screamed. 'Are you all right?' said a boy with a torch outside.

Kyle Ruscoe (9)
St Stephen's CE Primary School, Banks

The Magic Potion

I poured the last ingredient into my most important potion then suddenly *bang!* and I disappeared and landed in a faraway country. There was no one there, I was left alone. Then out the corner of my eye I saw a slight movement. I was scared. My mum appeared.

Sophie Stevens (9)
St Stephen's CE Primary School, Banks

The Volcano

Wibble, wobble, wibble, wobble.
'Argh, help don't let me fall!' screamed Chelsea.
As she stared down at the roaring hot volcano she sweated like mad.
'OK guys time's up you can carry on with the acts next week,' said the drama teacher over everyone's voice.
'Bye Miss,' Chelsea said happily.

Amy Gillow (9)
St Stephen's CE Primary School, Banks

The Spooky Night!

I was walking down the street, minding my own business. It was creepy. I could hear feet stomping towards me, then as I slowly turned my head, blood rushed to the tip of my tongue! I spotted a ... vampire! But then I realised it was Hallowe'en!

Lilyanna Rigby (9)
St Stephen's CE Primary School, Banks

The Journey To Atlantis

As I got onto the journey to Atlantis I was happy and relaxed. The journey was fine then suddenly it went dark and gloomy, we began to fall. My eyes shut, I screamed loudly then all of a sudden we stopped. I realised the ride had come to an end.

Leah Gearie (8)
St Stephen's CE Primary School, Banks

The Snowman

I woke up last Friday and it seemed brighter outside than usual. It had snowed heavily overnight. I ran outside and built a snowman. It took ages, I finished at teatime. The next morning he was gone, it had rained that night.

Connor Hancock (8)
St Stephen's CE Primary School, Banks

Rainbow

I was walking along the country grass and I saw a rainbow, a very light one. I ran towards the rainbow where I could see it. I finally got to the end of the rainbow. There was a pot of gold, I jumped in the pot and went, 'Yippee.'

Siobhan Glover (10)
St Teresa's Primary School, St Helen's

The Wrong Spell

There was a professor who did magic. He put a bit of this in and that but then he put the wrong potion in and then *Bang!* everything went in smoke. He cleared the smoke away and then he was young again. Then seconds later his mum shouted him, 'Peter … '

Daniel Shepherd (9)
St Teresa's Primary School, St Helen's

The Monster Cave

I'm home from school, home alone in the house. *Creak, crack* when the floorboard fell through. I landed in the cellar with a thud! Green eyes staring at me I had entered the monster's cave. He pushed me against the wall. The lights switched on.
'Happy Hallowe'en,' said my brother!

Natalie Devine (10)
St Teresa's Primary School, St Helen's

The Ghost

I was in the house just about to turn the TV on when I saw a ghost. It went upstairs then into a room. I opened the door, the light was off. Then the door slammed shut. I saw two big eyes and then my brother jumped out.

Katie Ellis (9)
St Teresa's Primary School, St Helen's

Night Ghost

I was getting into bed. My mum said, 'Night,' and went out, before I knew it I was asleep. I was having a dream. There in front of me was a ghost. I ran! Soon I hit a wall and it went black. I heard the whine of the ghost …

Daniel Eddleston (10)
St Teresa's Primary School, St Helen's

Doomed!

I was walking along a dark bridge, didn't know where it led. Eventually I got to the end. I saw a sign saying *Doomed*. From then I was scared. I walked over a couple of bumps and could hear a beeping noise and then *boom!* I died horribly.

Nathan Baines (10)
St Teresa's Primary School, St Helen's

Doom

I feel sick. Only five more minutes and then doom. I watch the clock and count down the seconds until - doom. Here I am, eleven years old and yet I am going to face - doom. The bell sounds and my name is announced. Here it is - doom. The dentist. No!

Beth Holmes (11)
Sound & District Primary School, Sound

No One's Home

Sara came home one day. Mum and Dad would not be home until five o'clock. She turned on the telly to her favourite program. Terrifying her, she heard someone scratching the door. Sara looked through the letterbox. Was someone there? She opened the door and there was Fluffy.

Leanne Read (10)
Sound & District Primary School, Sound

Hell Was Coming

Hell was coming. I stood there while it came for me. I had to go, it was right before my eyes. I stepped back, nearly fainting, but I was forced to go when I got on, the gates closed behind me … I hate going to Sound School on the bus.

Andrew Elson (10)
Sound & District Primary School, Sound

Aliens! There It Is Again!

Argh! Aliens! Aliens! It's a dark spooky night! There it is again! Gliding in the sky! Maybe it's spying on me! There's something at the window, what is it?
A spaceship?
'Jack! That's Isabel's birthday balloon hung on a satellite dish!'

Lucy Earls (9)
Sound & District Primary School, Sound

The UFO

'Hello this is Vanilla Fudge, reporting for BBC. Today, here at this cornfield, aliens will arrive! Wow, I think that's their spaceship … it is! They're coming nearer … They've landed … The doors are opening. They're coming out! Oh! … they're people from NASA trying out a UFO that they've made.'

Becky Hadwen (10)
Sound & District Primary School, Sound

Untitled

On a dark, scary night I was going to a big, tall house to do some science work. I got into a pitch-black room. I switched the light on. *Bang!* Something had exploded. No, I heard *surprise!* I remembered it was my birthday. Wo! Wo! Wo! Ye ha!

Connor Thundercliffe (10)
Sound & District Primary School, Sound

Hallowe'en Night

It was dark, night-time, Hallowe'en, people were knocking on doors but there was a strange noise coming from downstairs. So Mark crept downstairs trembling. *Creak,* he heard the noise *rumble, tumble, rumble.* He opened the kitchen door. Fear running through his spine ... Oh the washing machine was on.

Ollie Barnes (9)
Sound & District Primary School, Sound

Super Spell

Adding the powder carefully, she gently stirred the big wooden spoon. The dark midnight cauldron was bubbling rapidly. The spell was turning a magical blue. It steamed up - she waited for the ghastly mansion to fall down! That is a super spell. Too bad she exploded!

Katie Johnson (10)
Sound & District Primary School, Sound

Devil Dad

Having just got in bed I heard some floorboards go *eeek!* Ten seconds later my brother went, *'Argh!'* The house went silent, the floorboard creaked again, getting louder. My door opened, 'Oh no!' It was every eight-year-old's worst nightmare, a hug from your dad.

Jordan Edge (10)
Sound & District Primary School, Sound

One Day Too Soon

Alarm goes, oh no I'm late. Where is my sock? Hiding under the bed. That's my uniform on. Homework done, no time for food, the bus is coming, the bridge up. Oh no now it's going down. School at last. All shut - oh no, it's Sunday!

Connor McGowan (11)
South Walney Junior School, Walney

Street Wise

The wind blows through my hair, running footsteps, motors bustling, the smell of litter, sweets and dirty crisp wrappers. My hair ruffles as I turn my head left, right, left then right again, a sturdy sound then phew … ! I made it across the road safely and I'm on my way.

Rachel Pearce (11)
South Walney Junior School, Walney

Stolen!

My heart pounded in my chest like a Blacksmith's hammer connecting with an anvil. The tree scratched my face as I hid. The horses galloped by, hooves crashing against the ground, sending dust flying into my eyes. Clutching the stolen gold coins tightly. Phew, I got away with it!

Bradley Jepson-Leech (10)
South Walney Junior School, Walney

Fire

I saw smoke coming from my house. I phoned the fire brigade, who arrived just as I walked through the gate to see Dad cooking on the barbecue. 'Never mind,' said the firemen, 'it's our teatime.'

I apologised and Mum asked them to stay for tea. We all enjoyed ourselves.

Matthew Williamson (11)
South Walney Junior School, Walney

The Chase!

Running through the bushes to get out of sight, my heart beating like crazy. Puffed out of breath. But I couldn't stop now. Ducking branch from branch, I found the perfect place! Moving branches to keep hidden. I tried not to breathe, '49, 50, ready or not, here I come!'

Lauren Devlin (11)
South Walney Junior School, Walney

The Menacing Monster

Sweat covered my face as a shadowy figure slid into the room. I tightly pulled the cover over me. I slowly fell asleep. As I slowly re-awoke the beast stood silent but deadly. Then came a menacing cry, 'Daniel get out of bed, you will be late for school.'

Abby Long (10)
South Walney Junior School, Walney

The First Time!

Blackness surrounded me. Everybody screaming and wailing in confused disorientation. Was I in Hell? Now I was panicking and sobbing but amazingly daylight came into view. Hallelujah! I really wished I had listened to my mum when she stressed I was too young to ride the Black Hole in Blackpool.

Jayd Arnold (11)
South Walney Junior School, Walney

Loose Feet

My stomach was doing somersaults, my partner looked terrified. Somebody caught our attention. 'Now it's your turn girls.' My knees began to shake, I took a deep breath and entered the room. The music finished. I was glowing, my lips were smiling - I did it, I'd finished the dance competition.

Hannah Livesey (11)
South Walney Junior School, Walney

Hide-And-Seek

10 … 9 … 8 … 7 … running through the bushes as fast as I can. 6 … 5 … 4 … I'm panicking, rushing, gasping for breath. I can still hear the countdown 3 … 2 … 1 … I carry on searching, I find the perfect spot, I sit and wait. 'Here I come ready or not.'

Rebecca Murdoch (11)
South Walney Junior School, Walney

The Mystical Universe

I was in a universe of my own. Mystical beasts everywhere. It seemed a lifetime to me, many locals cheered as I battled through wind and rain, to destroy the dragon. More adventures await, but I'm being dragged out of this world. It ends, as I shut the book.

Callum Sparkes (11)
South Walney Junior School, Walney

Humpty Dumpty

Humpty Dumpty was alone. He climbed up a wall.
It became pitch-black. Humpty was scared. He started to swing on the wall whilst humming a tune. Swing, swing, swing. Humpty fell off the wall. All the king's horses and all the king's men said, 'Hey it's scrambled egg tonight.'

Emily Bosanko (11)
South Walney Junior School, Walney

Stalked

I felt the creature's breath on the back of my neck. Raising my sword I quickly turned and lashed out at the hideous creature stalking me. I recoiled in fear at the terrifying sight before me, death beckoned.
'Cut,' shouted the director.
'Brilliant, let's call it a day.'

Harry Winship (11)
South Walney Junior School, Walney

The Hero!

A brave man steps up from nowhere, with courage. Then defeats a monster barehanded, He ripped its arm, which hangs on a wall soon after, its mother had her head decapitated - (flesh ripping.) Furthermore, a sea serpent appeared. It was killed by the brave man. A hero was born - Beowulf.

Natasha Reay (11)
South Walney Junior School, Walney

The Big Fight

Fight! Fight! Fight! Round one of the match. Beowulf vs Grendal! Hero's eye catches Devil's eye … *Bang!* First move by Beowulf. Grendal swings, Beowulf ducks! *Whack!* Grendal's down! Beowulf wins!

Hours later, the king says to Beowulf, 'You are a brave man. You are our new king! You're the bravest!'

Natalie Jayne White (11)
South Walney Junior School, Walney

Hide-And-Seek

Diving into the bushes, I run, I hide. Trying to be as quiet as a mouse, as still as a statue. So they won't find me. I see others running, I hear more screaming. I stay very still and extremely quiet.
'1, 2, 3 ready or not, here I come!'

Sasha McCormick (11)
South Walney Junior School, Walney

The Chase

The bush rushing past me as I run as fast as my legs will carry me. I don't know how much time I have left. I can't believe they left me alone! Why now? Why here? Then suddenly I trip over a stone.

'3, 2, 1 - Here I come.'
'Caught.'

Jodie Evans (10)
South Walney Junior School, Walney

The Story Of Grendle

A baby born. Turned away by his people, then becomes a monster. Lurks away, killings start, can no one stop him? Happy warriors rejoice, he's dead. Even his family is in danger but destiny has said its last word, that's how it must be. He is not a monster anymore.

Phoebe Goulding (11)
South Walney Junior School, Walney

Flying

I belted up, my ears popped. I was on my way flying in the air. Rain, thunder, shaking me, trembling. The sky lit up with lightning. My only wish now was to land. I know with a thud, but I know I'll be starting my holiday. Yipee!

Joshua Francis (11)
South Walney Junior School, Walney

Night Of Terror

The moon was gleaming into the window - a magical shimmering unicorn. Disorientated, I was afraid of what was to come. Approaching the deep, black hallway. Something seemed to be following me. What was it? Suddenly a thunderous sound echoed around the room as I sprinted. My shadow was haunting me …

Vicky Rigg (11)
South Walney Junior School, Walney

Don't Give Up

I thought I'd never do it but my dad said I could if I kept on practising. I kept falling off, scraping my knees, losing my balance. I wanted to give up.
'Don't give up,' everyone kept saying.
In the end they were right, I can now ride my bike.

Rebecca Reid (10)
South Walney Junior School, Walney

The Mystery?

I was alone, the house was dark and empty. I was sure Mum and Dad would be back soon! I sat down to watch the telly - seconds, minutes, hours passed. They were still not home. The door opened, a black figure scarpered down the hall. *Who was it?* I wondered.

Hannah Faragher (11)
South Walney Junior School, Walney

Disappearance

'Where have they gone, all those ships?' She searched day and night, the scientist from her research vessel. The next day she searched again and this time she had luck. She saw the Atlantic eat a ship, this was the evidence she needed …

Catherine Stobart (10)
Welton Primary School, Carlisle

The Monster

Sian was asleep. She woke up and heard a sound. 'What is it?' she said. It got louder and louder. She was very scared. It jumped up and said, 'Hello.'
'Argh!'
Sian then realised it was her dad back from his holiday in Mexico. He was very, very, very brown.

Zoe Morris (8)
Welton Primary School, Carlisle

The Mystery Of The Night Monster

One dark stormy night a monster rose from beyond the grave in the Scottish Highlands. Steve saw it go over to the hill of the wolf boy. That night Steve couldn't sleep. He kept thinking that the monster would come after him.
'Wake up Steve, time for school.'
'Phew!'

Michael Studholme (10)
Welton Primary School, Carlisle

My Accident

Bing! The school bell rang. I started walking home. I looked left and right, before I carefully crossed the busy road. I was in the middle of the road when … *bang!* I was knocked down. Then I heard my mother's soft voice, I was in hospital with a broken ankle.

Megan Wetherell (11)
Welton Primary School, Carlisle

Dr Moss Experiment

Dr Moss wakes up at 7am. He goes out to meet Dr Miny. He gets to his lab and tries out a new experiment nobody has ever tried. When he had finished he realised it was poisoned. Luckily they were both wearing helmets. They were never the same again.

Sarah Wolstencroft (9)
Welton Primary School, Carlisle

Information

We hope you have enjoyed reading this book - and that you will continue to enjoy it in the coming years.
If you like reading and writing, drop us a line or give us a call and we'll send you a free information pack.
Alternatively visit our website at www.youngwriters.co.uk

Write to:
Young Writers Information,
Remus House,
Coltsfoot Drive,
Peterborough,
PE2 9JX
Tel: (01733) 890066
Email: youngwriters@forwardpress.co.uk